Stop the Picnic!

by Paul Medina
illustrated by Bob Barner

 HOUGHTON MIFFLIN   BOSTON

Printed in China

ISBN 10: 0-618-88646-X
ISBN 13: 978-0-618-88646-3

6789 0940 16 15 14 13
4500404702

It's picnic time!
The Ants are packed to go.

How many Ants are there?

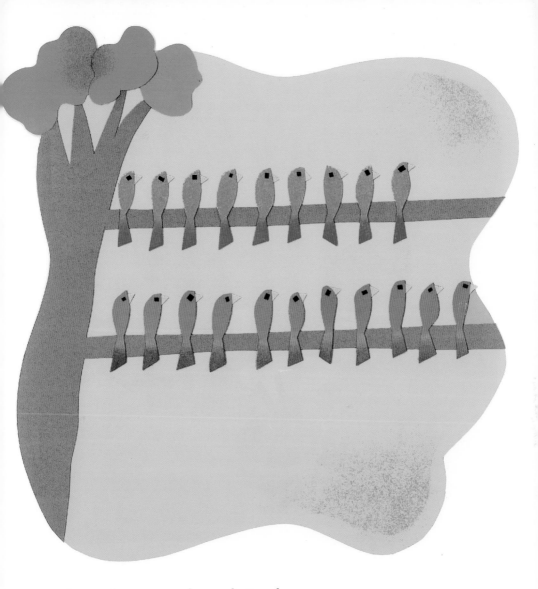

Look at the birds.

They will join the picnic!

Are there fewer blue birds or red birds?　　**3**

Look at the squirrels!
They bring acorns.

How many squirrels are there?

Strawberries! Blueberries!
They are so sweet.

Are there more blueberries or strawberries?   **5**

The picnic is not ready yet.
Two ants play while they wait.

Are there more yellow or blue flowers?

Oh, no! People!
The picnic is over !

How many people are there?

Join the Picnic

Draw Categorize and Classify
1. Look at page 7.
2. Draw a ✕ for each person.
3. Draw a ☐ for each ant.

Tell About
1. Look at page 3.
2. Tell someone how many more red birds there are.

Write
1. Look at page 4.
2. Write how many squirrels came to the picnic.